DEL REY
NEW YORK

Stay safe online. Any website addresses listed in this book are correct at the time of going to print. However, Del Rey is not responsible for content hosted by third parties. Please be aware that online content can be subject to change and websites can contain content that is unsuitable for children. We advise that all children are supervised when using the Internet. This publisher does not have any control over and does not assume any responsibility for author or third-party websites or their content.

ONLINE SAFETY FOR YOUNGER FANS
Spending time online is great fun! Here are a few simple rules to help younger fans stay safe and keep the Internet a great place to spend time:
- Never give out your real name—don't use it as your username.
- Never give out any of your personal details.
- Never tell anybody which school you go to or how old you are.
- Never tell anybody your password except a parent or a guardian.
- Be aware that you must be 13 or over to create an account on many sites. Always check the site policy and ask a parent or guardian for permission before registering.
- Always tell a parent or guardian if something is worrying you.

Published in the United States by Del Rey, an imprint of Random House, a division of Penguin Random House LLC, New York.

DEL REY and the HOUSE colophon are registered trademarks of Penguin Random House LLC.

Published in hardcover in the United Kingdom by Egmont UK Limited.

ISBN 978-1-101-96642-6
Ebook ISBN 978-1-101-96643-3

Printed in China on acid-free paper by C & C Offset

Written by Alex Wiltshire

Illustrations by Sam Ross

randomhousebooks.com

2 4 6 8 9 7 5 3 1

First US Edition

Design by Joe Bolder and Ant Duke

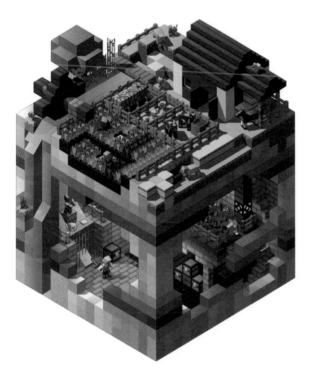

GUIDE TO:
⟩FARMING

CONTENTS

INTRODUCTION · 5
WHAT IS FARMING? · 6-7
FARMING BASICS · 8-9

1. FARMING CROPS

PRINCIPLES OF CROP FARMING · 12-13
WHEAT, CARROTS, POTATOES & BEETROOT · · · · · · · · · · · · · · · · · 14-23
MELONS AND PUMPKINS · 24-25
SUGAR CANES · 26-27
MUSHROOMS · 28-29
COCOA · 30-31

2. ANIMAL FARMING

PRINCIPLES OF ANIMAL FARMING · 34-35
PASSIVE MOBS · 36-39
TAMEABLE MOBS · 40-41

3. HOSTILE MOB FARMING

PRINCIPLES OF HOSTILE MOB FARMING · 44-47
EQUIPMENT · 48-49
OVERWORLD MOBS · 50-57
NETHER MOBS · 58-67

4. BLOCK FARMING

PRINCIPLES OF BLOCK FARMING · 70-71
BLOCKS · 72-77
FINAL WORDS · 78-79

INTRODUCTION

Welcome to the official *Guide to Farming*! There are many ways to play Minecraft, but one of the most satisfying is journeying through Survival mode to the End. Along the way you'll need many items and blocks, and creating them quickly and efficiently is what farming is all about.

Figuring out systems to do the work for you is fun, and they're fulfilling to watch in action. This guide shows you what you can produce, why you'd want to produce it, and how. It starts with growing crops and moves on to livestock, and then turns to farming hostile mobs, finally finishing with generating blocks.

As farming at its purest is about making the resources you need to survive and venture onward, the focus here is on farms that are practical, using few rare resources while being safe and straightforward to build and use. They're meant to be about making your Minecraft life easier, after all. But that doesn't mean you can't be a little creative and silly with them, too.

Let your inventive side loose, and enjoy!

OWEN JONES
THE MOJANG TEAM

WHAT IS FARMING?

In Survival mode you'll often find yourself needing special items, blocks and food in order to stay alive and to access new abilities and places. But you don't always have to go out on dangerous expeditions to find them. With a little ingenuity, you can make all the useful items you need, right at home.

CROPS

Learn ways of cultivating delicious crops, from simple field layouts to amazing automatic farming systems. And for when you've harvested your crops, find out what to make with them.

ANIMALS

Whether for their produce or their meat, it's always good to have animals around. You'll learn how to breed and bring up every domestic beast, and what they'll give you.

HOSTILE MOBS

Hostile mobs drop precious treasures and can even grant you experience when you kill them. Farming them takes great care and isn't for the faint of heart, but it will reap you big rewards.

BLOCKS

If you're a builder or landscaper with a mind to creating something huge, you can produce many of the materials you need to construct your vision instead of having to find them in the wild.

FARMING BASICS

To make the most of farming, it's very useful to have knowledge of some of the common tools, items, concepts and processes that it involves. Let's take a quick look at some key elements.

HOPPERS AND CHESTS

Many farming systems use hoppers to automatically collect produce and send them to a chest. They suck in any item that touches their top. To connect hoppers, first place the chest in which you want the produce to end up, then, while crouching, place a hopper on either its sides or above. Connect more hoppers as required, always while crouching. Remember that things can only go across or down through hoppers, never up.

REDSTONE

You'll soon find yourself needing redstone as you build your farming machines. When laid on blocks it forms wire, allowing you to connect things together, such as a lever to a piston. You find redstone ore in the lowest 16 layers of the world, in veins of 4 to 8 blocks. Each ore yields 4 or 5 redstone when mined with an iron pickaxe or better.

LIGHT

Many crops will only grow if there is enough light, and many mobs only appear in the dark. There are 16 levels of light. The brightest is 15, which is the Overworld's surface on a sunny day. The darkest is 0, when you can't see anything. A torch creates 14 light, but with each block's distance from a source of light, its brightness drops by one. So the block right next to a torch has a light value of 13, and the one next to that is 12. Consider light levels if crops are not growing or if mobs are not spawning.

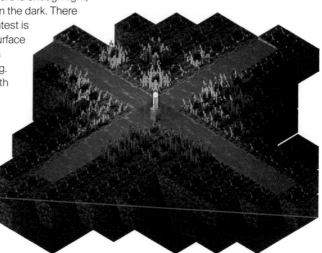

EXPERIENCE

Whenever you perform certain actions, such as defeating hostile mobs, mining ores and smelting, you earn experience. You can spend it on enchanting tools, weapons and armor with enchantment tables and anvils. Many enchantments make farming quicker, easier and more effective!

1

FARMING CROPS

In this section you'll learn what plants you can grow and how they'll feed you, how to bring in bumper harvests by planting perfect fields, and also how to construct amazing farming machines that will do all the hard work for you.

PRINCIPLES OF CROP FARMING

Growing your own food will save you hours of hunting for it or having to go hungry. Here's what you need to know to get started, and what tools and space will help you establish your fields and grow your crops successfully.

1 For most crops, fields should start as flat land with a surface layer of dirt blocks. Consider building them near a source of water for easy access.

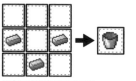

IRON BUCKET RECIPE

2 Most crops need water to grow at their full rate, so ensure you plant within 4 blocks of water. Without water nearby they'll still slowly grow, but any unused farmland will quickly revert to dirt. Dig channels and place water in them with a bucket.

3 To plant crops you'll need some seeds or the crops themselves. Wheat seeds drop from tall grass. Beetroot seeds can be found in chests in dungeons and abandoned mineshafts. Potatoes, beetroot and carrots are found growing in villages and potatoes and carrots are grown by planting one of the crops in farmland so it can produce more.

4 Most crops need a light level of 9 or higher in the block above them to grow, so your farm is best placed outside. Well-positioned torches can help your crops grow by night.

5 Each crop grows through various stages as it reaches maturity, which takes roughly 2 Overworld days. If you harvest too soon you won't get any produce, but you can speed growth up by feeding plants bone meal.

6 You'll need a hoe to plant seeds. Use it on dirt or grass blocks to till them into farmland, which is slightly lowered and has grooves that run across the top surface.

IRON HOE RECIPE

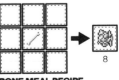

BONE MEAL RECIPE

8

13

WHEAT, CARROTS, POTATOES & BEETROOT

Wheat, carrots, potatoes and beetroot grow in similar ways, so they can be farmed together using the same farming methods. Let's take a look at how these crops behave, and how to grow them in the most efficient way.

WHEAT

One of the first crops you'll farm, wheat makes delicious baked products and can be used to breed cows, sheep, mooshrooms and tame horses (see pages 36-40).

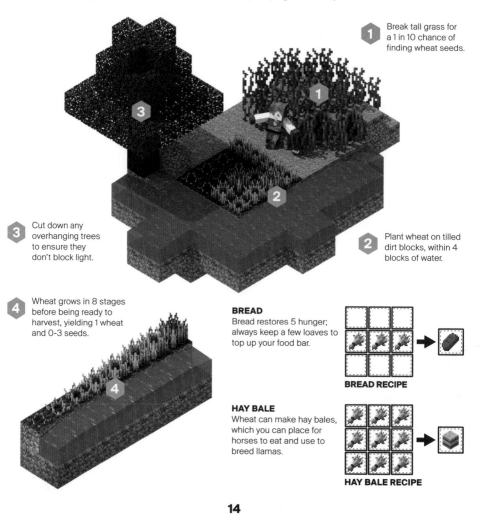

1 Break tall grass for a 1 in 10 chance of finding wheat seeds.

3 Cut down any overhanging trees to ensure they don't block light.

2 Plant wheat on tilled dirt blocks, within 4 blocks of water.

4 Wheat grows in 8 stages before being ready to harvest, yielding 1 wheat and 0-3 seeds.

BREAD
Bread restores 5 hunger; always keep a few loaves to top up your food bar.

BREAD RECIPE

HAY BALE
Wheat can make hay bales, which you can place for horses to eat and use to breed llamas.

HAY BALE RECIPE

CARROTS

You can use carrots to breed rabbits and pigs, or you can eat them yourself. Carrots are a useful food to farm, but they can be tricky to get hold of.

1 Find carrots in village fields and chests, and as rare drops from zombies.

2 Plant carrots within 4 blocks of water so they grow at full speed.

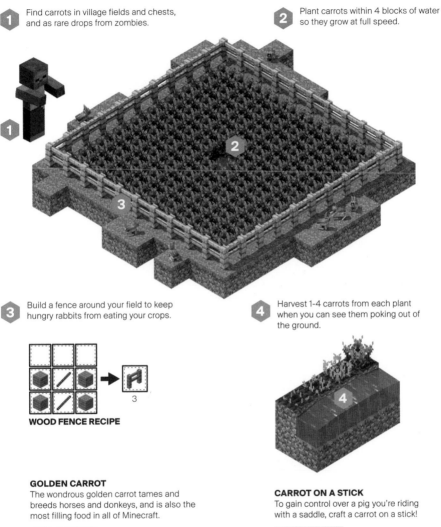

3 Build a fence around your field to keep hungry rabbits from eating your crops.

4 Harvest 1-4 carrots from each plant when you can see them poking out of the ground.

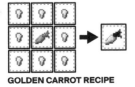

WOOD FENCE RECIPE

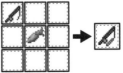

GOLDEN CARROT
The wondrous golden carrot tames and breeds horses and donkeys, and is also the most filling food in all of Minecraft.

GOLDEN CARROT RECIPE

CARROT ON A STICK
To gain control over a pig you're riding with a saddle, craft a carrot on a stick!

CARROT ON A STICK RECIPE

POTATO

This root vegetable is a good source of easy food because it doesn't need to be crafted with anything else to produce a nutritious meal.

 Villagers often farm potatoes and store them in their chests. They're also rare drops from zombies.

Harvest when you can see the roots protruding from the ground. Each crop will yield 1-4 potatoes.

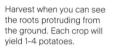

Trade between 15 and 19 potatoes for an emerald from brown-robed villagers. They can also buy most other crops.

BAKED POTATO

Bake a potato in your furnace to produce a meal that restores 5 hunger.

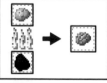

BAKED POTATO RECIPE

TIP

Watch out! Very rarely, poisonous potatoes drop as you harvest. You can recognize them by their green tinge. Eating one might poison you.

BEETROOT

Beetroot has several handy uses. You can give it to pigs to encourage them to breed, cook it to make soup, or use it to make red dye.

1 Beetroot grows in village fields and can also be found in chests.

2 Keep your crops growing at night by placing torches nearby.

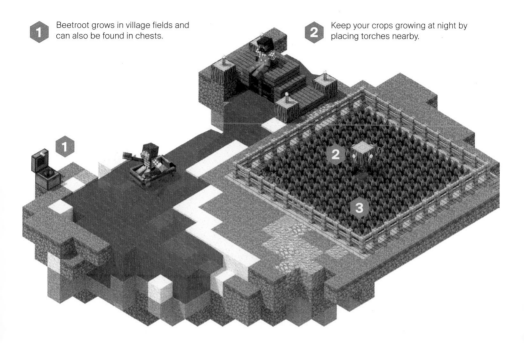

3 Plant beetroot seeds to grow them. Harvest from plants or find them in chests outside villages.

4 Each plant yields 1 beetroot and 0-3 beetroot seeds.

BONE MEAL

Bone meal can be used on most crops to speed up their growth. It's expensive for big fields but great for helping to gather plenty of crops to sow in the first stages of establishing your fields. Bones are dropped by skeletons and often found in chests. See pages 50-51 for how to farm them.

BEETROOT SOUP

Crafting beetroot with a bowl will give you beetroot soup which restores 6 hunger.

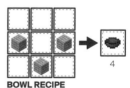

BOWL RECIPE

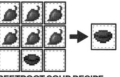

BEETROOT SOUP RECIPE

GROWTH MECHANICS

To farm wheat, carrots, potatoes and beetroot efficiently you need to understand how they grow, which means learning a little about how Minecraft works.

1 Things happen during each tick. Pistons move, your hunger bar decreases, plants grow. The game chooses three random blocks in every nearby "chunk," a 16 x 16-block area, 256 blocks high, and checks to see if it's possible for something to happen to them.

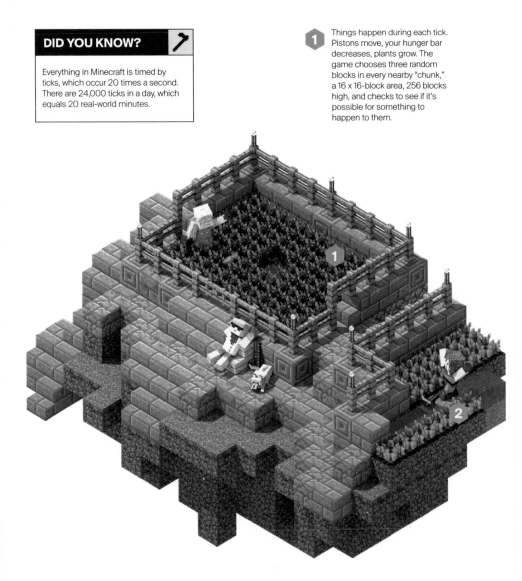

2 If the selected block is your carrot plant, there's a chance it will grow to its next stage of development if the light in the block above is 9 or more. This is more likely to happen if it's within 4 blocks of water, and if the blocks around it are hydrated farmland. But if the 8 blocks around the plant have the same plant growing in them, it becomes half as likely to grow, unless they are in a row.

GETTING YOUR FIELD STARTED

Using these rules, you can make an efficient field. It grows crops quickly and is useful when you're building up your supplies of seeds for new crops early in the game.

Plant your crops in rows.

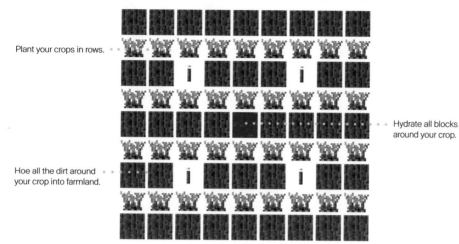

Hoe all the dirt around your crop into farmland.

Hydrate all blocks around your crop.

LATER GAME FIELD

Once you have lots of seeds and a choice of crops, fill in the gaps to use the space efficiently. This layout grows slightly slower, but you'll get more out of your farm in the long term.

Suspend blocks above the field with torches on each face so they don't take up space in the field.

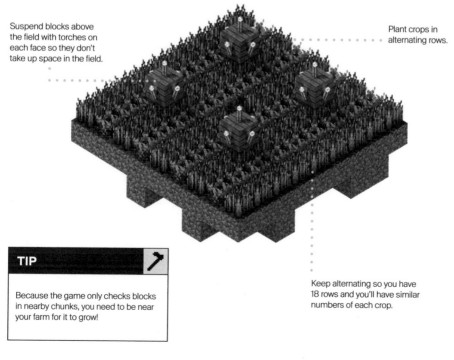

Plant crops in alternating rows.

TIP

Because the game only checks blocks in nearby chunks, you need to be near your farm for it to grow!

Keep alternating so you have 18 rows and you'll have similar numbers of each crop.

EFFICIENT FIELD DESIGN

This semi-automatic stacked wheat, carrot, potato and beetroot farm gets the most out of the available space and makes quick work of harvesting. If you need more fields, you can add as many levels as you like.

1 Plant crops in alternating rows for speedy growth (see previous page).

2 Place water below the glass at the edge of each field to irrigate the land.

3 Harvest each level by pulling the lever, which moves a line of pistons, releasing water from the level above.

YOU WILL NEED:

4 The flood washes over the field, breaking all the plants and pushing the produce to the bottom of the field for easy collection.

5 Glass blocks prevent the water and produce from washing over the side and the fences prevent mobs from getting in.

6 Pull the lever again to stop the flood, collect the produce, and replant the field for your next crop.

TIP >

Use item frames to hold the crop you're farming and display them next to your fields so you know what's growing!

MOJANG STUFF 🄫

With the Update Aquatic, the behavior of water is changing slightly to make it easier to build structures underwater. We don't want to break old contraptions that use fences to block flowing water - but now if you place a fence inside a water source block, the water will move through it.

FULLY AUTOMATIC FARM

Wheat, carrots, beetroot and potatoes need to be replanted after each harvest, so it's difficult to completely automate your farms. One way it can work is with farmer villagers, who plant and harvest fields. But it takes a lot of preparation to get it going.

BUILD YOUR COLLECTION SYSTEM

With its pockets full, your villager will leave produce on the field as it harvests. A minecart with a hopper inside it running below the field will gather them and deposit them in a chest.

1 Design a rail layout that exactly matches the shape and size of the field you'll build above it.

2 Powered rails keep the minecart moving. Place one every 10 blocks or so along the track and power them from below with levers.

3 Light any areas where mobs may spawn, and enclose the track with a fence to prevent spiders from getting inside and stopping the minecart.

4 Craft a minecart with a hopper inside it; as it runs up and down the track it collects items on the block above at a rate of 20 per second and deposits them in a chest at the end.

YOU WILL NEED:

HIRE A VILLAGER

Finding the right kind of villager and getting it to work for you can be difficult.

Brown-robed farmer villagers will tend crops, planting and harvesting when they're mature. Your field needs to be at least 32 blocks from the edge of any village so the villager doesn't try to return home. A way of moving a villager is pushing them into a minecart in their village and building a track to your field.

To tend crops, villagers need to carry seeds. To prevent them from picking up harvested produce, you need to fill their 8 inventory slots. Collect 8 stacks (64 items) of wheat and beetroot seeds, carrots and potatoes and drop them by your villager so it picks them up.

PREPARE YOUR FIELD

This is where the magic happens! Get the villager in place and wait for it to start working. Remember to return to your field to give your villager more seeds.

1 Build your field 1 block above your track so the minecart runs directly below.

2 Hoe the dirt into farmland and the villager will begin planting.

3 Ensure the field is fully fenced in so the villager cannot escape and mobs cannot get inside.

YOU WILL NEED:

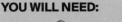

MELONS AND PUMPKINS

These vine-based fruit-bearing plants grow in very similar ways. Both grow fruit that provides good food, but pumpkins can also be crafted into snow golems and can even be worn in place of a helmet.

 1 Plant pumpkin or melon seeds in farmland. Get seeds by breaking the stems of parent plants. Pumpkins are found growing on grass across the Overworld, and melons naturally grow in jungles.

 2 Ensure water is within 4 blocks and that the location is bright so the stems grow at top speed.

5 When you harvest melons and pumpkins, new fruit will grow in the same spot without you having to replant your crops.

 4 Melons drop 3-7 melon slices when harvested. Each restores 5 hunger.

 3 Leave at least 1 empty block of dirt next to each plant for the fruit to grow into. The more empty dirt around the stem, the sooner you'll see fruit.

GOLEM GETTER
Build friendly golems with your pumpkins.

IRON GOLEM TEMPLATE

SNOW GOLEM TEMPLATE

EFFICIENT PLANTING

This layout gives a high chance of each of the dirt blocks being filled with a melon or pumpkin, while keeping the blocks with stalks hydrated.

Ensure your farm is fully lit.

You can repeat this pattern to make big fields, but make sure there are always two rows of dirt together and two rows of stalks.

Harvest crops with an axe, taking care not to hit the stalks.

AUTOMATIC MELON AND PUMPKIN FARM

This automatic farm doesn't grow produce fast, but is compact and can be left to itself to run.

When the melon or pumpkin block grows, it completes a redstone circuit and pushes a piston.

It can be stacked as high as you like.

Remember to place water next to your pumpkin.

A torch will help speed up growth at night.

The piston breaks the melon/pumpkin block and the produce is collected by 3 hoppers on each level.

Connect hoppers in a backward S shape like this, to a chest at the bottom.

YOU WILL NEED:

SUGAR CANES

These tall plants will allow you to craft paper, from which you can make books and maps. They'll also allow you to craft sugar, enabling you to create sweet delicacies like pumpkin pie, brew potions and heal horses if fed directly to them.

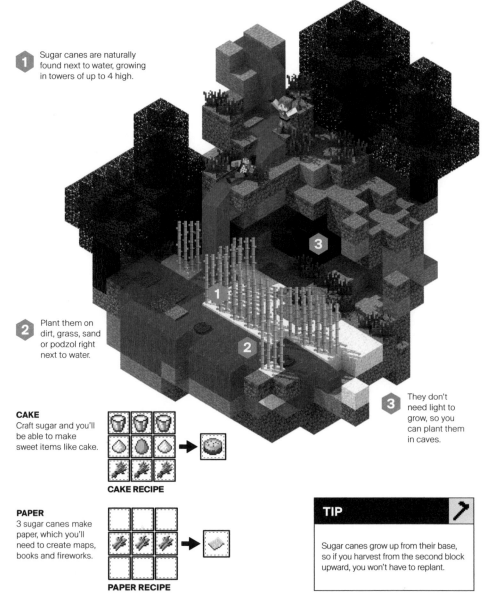

1 Sugar canes are naturally found next to water, growing in towers of up to 4 high.

2 Plant them on dirt, grass, sand or podzol right next to water.

3 They don't need light to grow, so you can plant them in caves.

CAKE
Craft sugar and you'll be able to make sweet items like cake.

CAKE RECIPE

PAPER
3 sugar canes make paper, which you'll need to create maps, books and fireworks.

PAPER RECIPE

TIP

Sugar canes grow up from their base, so if you harvest from the second block upward, you won't have to replant.

AUTOMATIC SUGAR CANES FARM

This simple machine uses the observer block to harvest sugar canes into a chest.

2 An observer block detects when the left-most sugar canes grow 3 blocks high.

1 Water flows from source blocks and along the planted row of sugar canes so they grow.

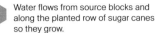

4 The broken sugar canes fall into the water, which washes them into hoppers connected to a chest.

MOJANG STUFF

Originally, sugar canes were just reeds, their only purpose being to create paper for books. We rebranded them as sugar canes to increase their number of (delicious) uses!

3 Pistons then push the full second row of sugar canes into the water, leaving a row to begin growing again.

YOU WILL NEED:

MUSHROOMS

Not all crops need light in order to thrive. Some, like the mushroom, prefer the darkness. This fungus makes nourishing soup and stew, and is also an important ingredient for many useful potions.

1 Look for red and brown mushrooms in any dark place, including under trees and in caves.

2 Plant small mushrooms on dirt that isn't exposed to the sky and has a light level of under 12, or on podzol or mycelium, where they will even grow outside in the day.

3 Mushrooms will spread if there are fewer than 5 in a 9 x 9 area.

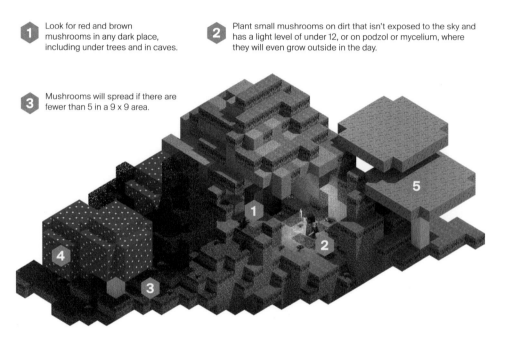

4 Huge mushrooms naturally grow in forests, swamps and on mushroom islands. Breaking their blocks will give you 0-2 small mushrooms.

5 Create huge mushrooms by using bone meal on a small mushroom. Ensure it has lots of space above and around it to grow into.

FERMENTED SPIDER EYE

Mushrooms are needed to craft fermented spider eye, which forms the base for a range of harming potions, including slowness and weakness and invisibility. Fermented spider eye can be crafted from a mushroom, sugar and a spider eye.

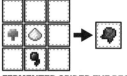

FERMENTED SPIDER EYE RECIPE

MUSHROOM STEW

Mushroom stew is a simple and very nutritious meal crafted from a brown mushroom, a red mushroom and a bowl.

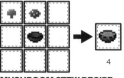

MUSHROOM STEW RECIPE

28

MUSHROOM FARM

The tricky thing about mushrooms is that mobs tend to spawn where they're growing. However, with clever lighting you can keep the level low enough for growing but high enough to prevent spawning.

1 The light level at floor level is never higher than 12 so mushrooms will grow.

2 Mushrooms spread in a very random fashion, and so it's difficult to design a space- and work-efficient farm.

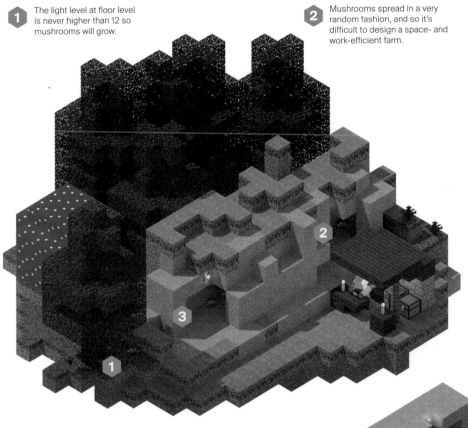

3 Build out corridors to increase your yields. Water flushing systems can break the crops and deposit them where you want.

The light level in the tunnel never goes below 10, so mobs cannot spawn.

DID YOU KNOW?

Use shears on a mooshroom and it'll drop mushrooms. Weird!

YOU WILL NEED:

COCOA

Deep in the jungle you'll find cocoa pods growing on tree trunks. They drop cocoa beans when mined, which produce chocolate and can be used to make lots of brown items and blocks, from fireworks to concrete.

1 Find cocoa growing on jungle trees; break to get cocoa beans.

2 Plant beans on jungle wood, which begin small and green and grow larger and browner as they mature. They don't need light to grow.

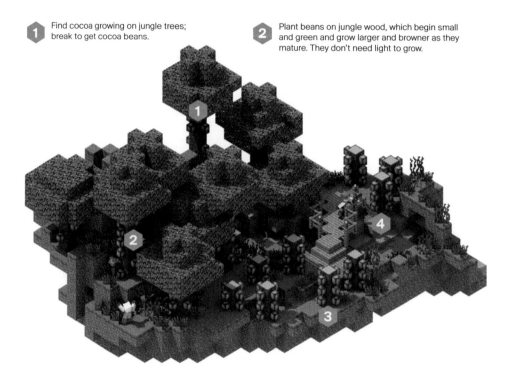

3 When creating wooden towers to grow cocoa, leave a block of space adjacent to each face for the cocoa pod to grow into.

4 Harvesting when unripe drops 1 cocoa bean; the third and final growth stage drops 2-3 cocoa beans.

COOKIES
Cookies restore 2 hunger, but don't feed them to parrots! They'll instantly die. You'll need wheat and cocoa beans to craft.

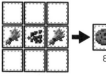

COOKIE RECIPE

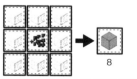

BROWN STAINED-GLASS RECIPE

TIP 〉

You can craft cocoa beans with glass, wool and many other colored items to make them brown.

30

EFFICIENT PLANTING

Cocoa beans will only grow on jungle wood, but it's quite simple to farm them in an efficient layout that packs lots in.

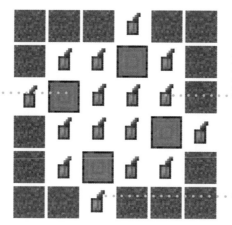

This pattern uses space very efficiently because each tree and its cocoa fits into each other.

Build each wooden "pole" 3 blocks high so you can reach the top cocoa pods from the ground for easy harvesting.

It's a quick and easy farm to build, but crops are slow to harvest.

COCOA WATER WALL

This structure uses water from a reservoir of water above to wash the mature beans down for easy harvesting.

 The jungle wood wall can be as long as you need.

2 The lever controls two walls of pistons that, when retracted, allow water from the central reservoir to run down the sides of the wall.

3 Trenches prevent the water from creating a large pool. Consider adding hoppers to collect the cocoa.

YOU WILL NEED:

ANIMAL FARMING

We turn now to the art of farming passive mobs, which are the source of many useful items and food, as well as experience points. We'll look at how to breed and keep livestock and how to gather their produce.

PRINCIPLES OF ANIMAL FARMING

Many passive mobs supply food and other useful items. Once you have a herd (or flock, pack or parcel) you can produce lots of items. Breeding can take time and requires knowledge and access to each mob's favorite foods, so it's a good idea to make a crop farm first.

FENCING

You'll need to keep your livestock from wandering, especially if they're hunted by predators, such as chicken-loving ocelots. Fences are ideal because no mob can jump over them, but you can see through them and easily get inside by placing gates.

LEADING

Most mobs will follow you if you're holding the food that is required to breed them. This comes in handy when you want to guide them into your paddocks.

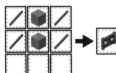

FENCE RECIPE

FENCE GATE RECIPE

BUTCHERING

Most livestock mobs are a source of meat, some of the most nutritious food around, and that means killing them. Meat should be cooked in a furnace before eating, though if a mob is killed by fire it will drop cooked meat.

SPACE

If there are too many mobs in a space enclosed by a fence, they'll begin to pop through it. If enclosed by solid blocks, they'll start to suffocate and die.

BREEDING

Most adult mobs produce offspring when a pair is fed a specific item of food, awarding 1-7 XP. Their children take around 20 minutes to reach adulthood, but if fed their species' breeding food, their growing time is cut by 10%. It usually takes 5 minutes before parents can breed again.

PASSIVE MOBS

Passive mobs can be seen wandering across the Overworld, often in grassy areas. Let's take a look at their behavior, what each mob drops, and the best way to go about collecting those drops.

CHICKEN

Spawning in grassy areas, adult chickens lay 1 egg every 5 to 10 minutes, which can be crafted into pumpkin pies and cake. Cooked chicken restores 6 hunger. Ocelots will hunt chickens.

BREEDING

Feed a pair of chickens with seeds, melon seeds, pumpkin seeds or beetroot seeds, or you can quickly grow a big flock by throwing eggs. 1 in 8 will successfully spawn a chick, and 1 in 32 of those will hatch into 4 chicks, which grow faster if fed seeds.

EGG FACTORY

This machine makes it much simpler to gather eggs from a large flock of chickens. It uses water to wash the eggs to one place.

DROPS WHEN ALIVE

∞

DROPS WHEN DEFEATED

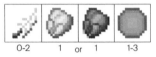

0-2	1	or 1	1-3

The chickens' living space is enclosed by fences so they can't fly out. For larger flocks, you can make the area bigger. Leave an open gap at the bottom for the water to flow through.

Use a water bucket to place water source blocks at the top of the structure.

Find as many eggs as you can and throw them inside. 1 in 8 will hatch.

Collect eggs from the water runway at the bottom.

PUMPKIN PIE RECIPE

YOU WILL NEED:

COW

Cows spawn in herds of between 4 and 8 in grassy areas. They are important as a source of leather for crafting armor and books. Use a bucket on a cow and it will be filled with milk.

BREEDING

Give wheat to 2 adult cows standing near each other to encourage them to breed.

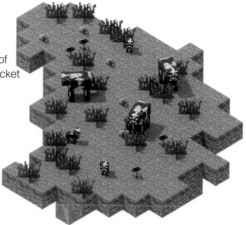

DROPS WHEN ALIVE

∞

DROPS WHEN DEFEATED

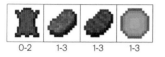

| 0-2 | 1-3 | 1-3 | 1-3 |

TIP	7

Fence a cow into a 1 x 2 block area near your home so you can easily milk it!

MOOSHROOM

Found only in the mushroom island biome, mooshrooms behave like cows but use a bowl on one and it will be filled with mushroom stew. Shear one and it will drop 5 mushrooms and turn into a cow.

BREEDING

Mooshrooms can only be bred with their own kind, not cows. Use wheat on a pair.

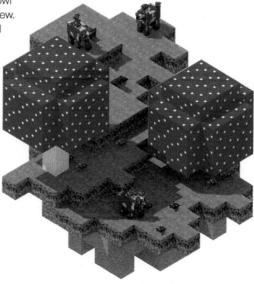

DROPS WHEN ALIVE

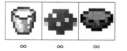

∞   ∞   ∞

DROPS WHEN DEFEATED

| 0-2 | 1-3 | 1-3 | 1-3 |

PIG

Found in grassy areas in rough groups of 4, pigs are a great source of nutritious food. Their porkchops restore 8 hunger.

BREEDING

Feeding carrots, potatoes or beetroot to a pair of pigs will create a piglet.

DROPS WHEN DEFEATED

1-3   or   1-3   1-3

RABBIT

Rabbits live in grasslands, deserts and ice plains in groups of an adult and 2 babies. Their meat restores 5 hunger. Their hides can only be crafted into leather, but 1 in 10 will drop a rabbit's foot, which, when brewed with awkward potions, will give you potion of leaping.

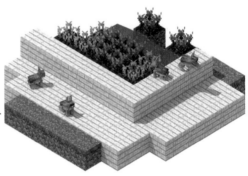

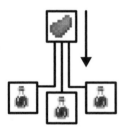

POTION OF LEAPING BREWING RECIPE

DROPS WHEN DEFEATED

0-1   0-1   or   0-1   0-1   1-3

BREEDING

Feed a carrot or a dandelion to adult rabbits to get them to breed. The baby rabbit's fur will match that of one of its parents, or there's a 5% chance it will match the biome you're in. To maximize the chance of breeding rabbits with specific fur, ensure both parents have it.

SHEEP

Sheep spawn on grass. Their mutton fills 6 hunger, but they're most useful as a source of wool. Most are white, but there's a 5% chance one will spawn as light gray, dark gray or black, and there's a 1 in 600 chance it will be pink. You can also dye them. Shear a sheep to gather 1-3 wool of its color; it will need to eat tall grass or a grass block before its wool will regrow.

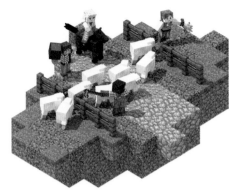

BREEDING

Feed wheat to a pair of sheep. If their wool color is compatible, their lamb will be a mix of both, so red and yellow parents will have an orange lamb. Otherwise, the lamb will be one of its parents' colors.

DROPS WHEN DEFEATED

	1-2 or	1-2	1-3
1			

DROPS WHEN ALIVE

∞

TIP

Sheep are hunted by wild wolves, so keep them protected behind fences.

SHEARING STATION

This structure makes shearing easy, collecting the wool in a chest.

1 The floor of the station is grass so the sheep can feed and regrow their wool.

3 Stand on this walkway and shear the sheep from above.

2 Pull a lever so pistons open the reservoir at the back and flush the sheep to the front.

4 Hoppers collect the wool and drop them in the connected chest.

YOU WILL NEED:

TAMEABLE MOBS

These mobs are a little more complicated than passive mobs – they'll need to be tamed before you can breed them or use them for any other purpose. Let's take a look at where they're found and how to earn their trust.

HORSE

Horses and donkeys roam savannas and plains. Once tamed by attempting to ride them until they stop trying to throw you off, they can perform several useful functions for farmers. Once given a saddle you can control them while riding, and donkeys and mules (which are not found in the wild and can only be bred) are smaller and stockier and can be given a chest so they'll carry goods.

BREEDING

Once tamed, horses can be bred with golden apples and carrots. Their foal's species depends on its parents, so two horses will have a horse, and a horse and donkey will birth a mule. The foal will need to be tamed. Speed up its growth with (from least to most effective): sugar, wheat, apple, golden carrot, hay bale, or golden apple.

DROPS WHEN DEFEATED

0-2   1-3

CAT

Cats are tamed from ocelots, which are found in jungles. They deter creepers from coming close, so they can help protect your farm from explosions. Taming is a delicate process: hold raw salmon or raw fish near an ocelot and wait as it approaches. It will be frightened away by any sudden movement. Cats follow their owner but can be commanded to sit to stay in place.

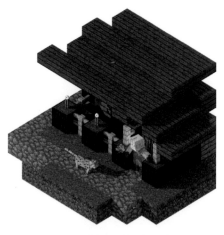

BREEDING

Feed raw salmon or raw fish to a pair of cats and they will produce a kitten, which will have the coloring of one of its parents.

DROPS WHEN DEFEATED

1-3

LLAMA

Llamas are native to savannas. Once tamed, they can be ridden but can't be controlled. Once equipped with a chest they're a great pack animal. A llama will carry 3, 6, 9, 12, or 15 slots, depending on its strength rating. Use a lead on a llama and all nearby llamas will form into a caravan.

TIP

Give your strongest llama a distinctive carpet to wear so you can easily identify it.

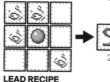

LEAD RECIPE

Leads can be crafted from a slimeball and string.

DROPS WHEN DEFEATED

0-2   1-3

BREEDING

Use hay bales on two tamed adults. The baby llama's strength will be influenced by its strongest parent's strength, so to get a strong pack, always breed with your strongest llama to raise your chances of having strong babies. Hay bales can be crafted from wheat.

WOLF

Wild wolves live in taiga biomes in packs of 4. Neutral to players, they can be tamed so that they will faithfully follow you, attacking skeletons and any other mobs that attack you. To tame, feed a wolf bones until a collar appears and its eyes change to look friendlier.

BREEDING

Feed a pair of tame wolves any kind of meat other than fish, such as raw beef, and they will produce a baby wolf.

DID YOU KNOW?

You can tell how healthy your wolf is by how high it holds its tail. Heal it by feeding it meat.

DROPS WHEN DEFEATED

1-3

HOSTILE MOB FARMING

Many hostile mobs drop wonderfully useful items that will aid you on your journeys, as well as experience points. But hunting these foes can be arduous as well as dangerous. In this section we'll look at how to farm hostile mobs safely.

PRINCIPLES OF HOSTILE MOB FARMING

Hostile mobs are the source of valuable and sometimes vital items that will aid you in your quest to defeat the ender dragon. Learning how to farm them often means embarking on complex constructions, but they're worth the work.

KILLING

Hostile mobs only drop certain items if they're killed by a player (or their wolf), so many farms collect live mobs for you to kill them manually. But there's a limit to the number of hostile mobs that can be around. To maximize the output of your farms, you'll need to kill them quickly to keep fresh mob spawns flowing.

SPAWNING

Your farm depends on mobs spawning. Because they only spawn in the area around you, you need to be near your farm for it to work.

MOJANG STUFF

Normally, only certain kinds of mobs spawn from spawners (and some, like cave spiders, *only* spawn from spawners) but if you use commands, you can use them to split out any mob - even forcing them to ride one another in weird combinations.

LIGHT

To get mobs spawning quickly where you want them to be, you need to stop them from spawning elsewhere. Ensure there are no dark places in hidden caverns within range and light up open ground or cover with slabs to prevent them from appearing outside your farm.

THE NETHER

Some hostile mobs only spawn in the Nether, so to farm them you'll need to set up a base so you can live there. However, many Overworld farming techniques, such as those that use water, won't work there.

SPAWNERS

Spawners found in dungeons, abandoned mineshafts, mansions, strongholds and fortresses are an excellent way of generating hostile mobs. If you find one, consider not destroying it so you can use it.

SPAWNING

Hostile mobs spawn according to a set of rules, and understanding these rules can help you build clever farms. Let's take a look at the factors that will affect the spawn rate of hostile mobs.

1 IS A PLAYER NEARBY?
There must be no players and no active beds within a sphere of a 24-block radius around the location the mob is trying to spawn.

2 WHAT BLOCK IS IT SPAWNING ON?
The block below the hostile mob must be opaque and have a solid top. That means it can be a solid block, like cobblestone or a block of iron (but not bedrock). It can be a slab, but only if it's aligned with the top of its layer, or stairs if they're upside down.

5 SPAWNERS
Mob spawners behave differently than standard spawning. They only activate if a player is within 16 blocks.

0	**0-24**	**24-32**		**32-128**
	NO MOBS SPAWN			**MOBS DESPAWNING**

24 BLOCKS OUT
Mobs spawn

32 BLOCKS OUT
Mobs begin despawning

IS THERE ENOUGH FREE SPACE?

3 Each hostile mob needs a certain amount of clear space around the spawning point. Most require a 2-block-high space, but spiders need 1 vertical block and 3 lateral blocks, and endermen need 3 vertical blocks. These blocks must be free of liquids, rails and solid blocks.

IS IT DARK ENOUGH?

4 Most mobs only spawn in blocks below light level 8, but some, like blazes, can spawn in brighter conditions. The darker the block is, the more likely the spawn will succeed. Direct sunlight makes it a lot more likely the spawn will fail.

DESPAWNING

Mobs also despawn - which means that they disappear from the world - according to a set of rules.

1. For mobs that haven't been within 32 blocks of a player for more than 30 seconds, every second there is a 1 in 40 chance it will despawn.

2. If players are more than 128 blocks from a mob in any direction, it will despawn immediately.

3. If the hostile mob is named with a name tag, or if it has picked up any items dropped by a player, it will not despawn.

MOJANG STUFF

If you use a name tag on a mob it becomes persistent and will never despawn. This can be handy: if you find a zombie villager, you can name them, lock them up, and venture off far and wide in search of the cure.

6

WHERE IS IT?

6 Only certain mobs spawn in the Overworld, Nether and End. Additionally, some mobs can only spawn in certain layers and generated locations. Witch huts only spawn witches. Only slime chunks can spawn slimes, and they must either be below layer 40 or in a swamp between layer 51 and 69.

128

128 BLOCKS OUT
All mobs despawn immediately

EQUIPMENT

Farming hostile mobs can be difficult and dangerous, but you can make your work easier and more profitable by investing in some special equipment and items.

DIAMOND SWORD

Because a lot of mob farms require you to do the killing, you need a strong and durable sword to make quick work of it. That means diamond.

Diamond ore is rare and is only found in small seams from levels 5 to 20 in the Overworld, so you will need to dig deep beneath the surface. It's most common between levels 12 to 16.

Mining with TNT can find diamond quickly. Once you have your simple mob farm set up (see page 51) you'll start quickly collecting gunpowder from creepers. Place a TNT block every 5 blocks around level 14, detonate, then examine the holes for seams of diamond ore. Watch out for lava floods!

ENCHANTMENTS

Improve your equipment for better drops and quicker killing with enchantments. Place up to 15 bookshelves around your enchantment table to increase its power. Offered enchantments depend on your level; the list is reset every time you enchant something. Pay for each enchantment with XP and lapis lazuli. Or use an anvil to apply enchanted books to your equipment and combine enchanted items.

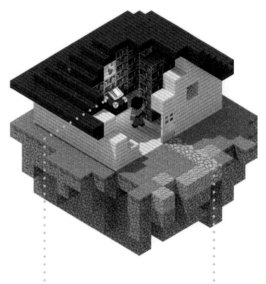

Enchantment tables can be crafted from obsidian, diamond and a book.

Anvils can be crafted from iron ingots and solid blocks of iron.

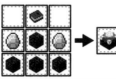

ENCHANTMENT TABLE RECIPE

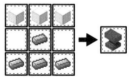

ANVIL RECIPE

LOOTING

To get the most drops from mobs and to raise the chances of their rare drops appearing, enchant your sword with looting. You'll get one extra drop for each level of enchantment, up to level III.

SILK TOUCH

This allows you to pick up some items that are normally destroyed when their block is broken, e.g., cobwebs (useful for the blaze farm on pages 62-65) and ice (see page 75).

UNBREAKING

Unbreaking raises the durability of your equipment, up to level III. It's best used on your enchanted diamond sword.

SHARPNESS

Sharpness increases the damage of your melee (hand-to-hand) attacks, with a level V sharpness doing 1.5 hearts of extra damage. Level V is only reached with the use of an anvil.

SMITE

Smite raises the damage you do to undead mobs, like zombies and skeletons, with level V smite doing 6.5 hearts of extra damage. It's excellent for killing wither skeletons.

POTIONS

Become more powerful or deal damage to groups of mobs by quaffing potions made at a brewing stand. You'll need many items to get the potions you want, including glass bottles, water, Nether wart, fermented spider eyes and gunpowder.

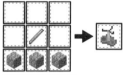

BREWING STAND RECIPE

A brewing stand can be crafted from cobblestone and a blaze rod.

POTION OF STRENGTH
Increases melee damage by 1.5 hearts for either 3 or 8 minutes.

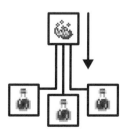

SPLASH POTION OF HARMING
Throw to do instant damage to groups of mobs, though it heals undead mobs. I: 3 hearts; II: 6 hearts.

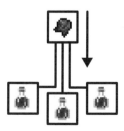

SPLASH POTION OF HEALING
Throw to do instant damage to groups of undead mobs.

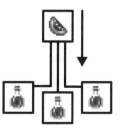

OVERWORLD MOBS

The Overworld is home to a variety of hostile mobs. They all pose unique threats and drop different valuable items. Let's take a look at each mob and learn how they can be farmed so you can collect as many of their drops as possible.

SKELETON

SPAWNS
In the Overworld on blocks under light level 8, and in Nether fortresses. In snowy biomes, most skeletons will be strays, which have a 50% chance of dropping an arrow tipped with slowness.

DROPS WHEN DEFEATED

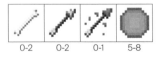

0-2	0-2	0-1	5-8

Arrows are useful, but all farmers treasure the bone meal that is crafted from skeleton bones. This wonder substance makes most crops grow faster.

ZOMBIE

SPAWNS
In the Overworld in groups of 4 on blocks under light level 8, or in groups of up to 20 near large villages at midnight. 1 in 20 zombies is a baby, which is smaller, faster and gives more XP.

DROPS WHEN DEFEATED

0-2	0-1	0-1	0-1	5-12

Rotten flesh will poison you if you eat it, but it has two other uses: it heals and tames wolves, and villagers can trade it for emeralds. Potatoes, carrots and iron ingots are rare drops. They also drop any armor or weapons they are holding.

SIMPLE MOB FARM

This farm collects items from zombies, skeletons, creepers, witches and spiders, using gravity to do the dirty work. It requires a lot of blocks but is so simple it can be built very early in your journey.

TIP

To collect XP as well as items, reduce the fall height to 22 blocks; mobs will survive the fall and most will die with a single punch.

1 Mobs spawn in the upper chamber. Open trapdoors trick them into thinking they can walk on them.

2 Light the top of the structure and the area at the bottom as well so hostile mobs can't spawn, maximizing spawns inside the chamber and minimizing danger.

3 Mobs fall through into 8-block-long channels of water that flow to a drop of 23 blocks.

5 Slabs prevent spiders that survive the fall from escaping. Anything not killed, including witches, which require a 32-block fall to die, can be finished off from safety.

4 Most mobs are killed by the fall. Hoppers at the bottom collect their items.

YOU WILL NEED:

SPIDER

SLIME

SPAWNS

In the Overworld on blocks under light level 8 in spaces of 1 block and higher, or from spawners. The common spider's smaller and poisonous relative, the cave spider, only spawns from spawners in abandoned mineshafts.

DROPS WHEN DEFEATED

| 0-2 | 0-1 | 5 |

String is handy for crafting bows, fishing rods and leads, and can be placed as a block to create tripwires. Spider eyes are poisonous if eaten but are crucial for brewing various potions, including poison, slowness, invisibility, harming and weakness. Note that spiders only drop eyes when killed by a player, not if killed by fall damage.

SPAWNS

Slimes spawn in random areas in the Overworld at level 40 and below at any light level, and in swamps at normal ground level at light level of under 8. Slimes come in three sizes; larger slimes split into smaller ones when they're defeated. Only the smallest slimes drop slimeballs when defeated.

DROPS WHEN DEFEATED

| 0-2 | 1-4 |

Slimeballs are handy items, used to craft leads, sticky pistons and magma cream (needed to brew potions of fire resistance), as well as the bouncy slime block.

DID YOU KNOW? >

Spiders' ability to climb walls means they often survive drop-trap farms.

DID YOU KNOW? >

If a charged creeper, a creeper superpowered by a lightning bolt, kills a zombie, skeleton or creeper, it will drop its head as an item!

CACTUS SLIME TRAP

If you can find a place where slimes spawn, this trap will use their stupidity to gather lots of slimeballs. It will also work for magma cubes in the Nether.

1 Find an area in a swamp or below level 40 where slimes spawn. If underground, you'll need to carefully mine out an area and note where slimes are appearing from.

2 Create a square chamber measuring around 30 blocks across. Light it well to prevent other mobs from spawning.

3 Plant a 3-block-high cactus on sand in the middle. The floor-level hoppers collect the slimeballs and send them to a chest.

5 Slimes hate iron golems and will try to attack them. But as they throw themselves at your bait, they'll bounce against the cactus and be killed!

4 On top of the cactus, place a block or slab and craft an iron golem on it, then surround it with a fence so it can't fall off.

YOU WILL NEED:

CREEPER

WITCH

SPAWNS
Anywhere in the Overworld on blocks of under light level 8.

DROPS WHEN DEFEATED

| 0-2 | 0-1 | 5 |

Gunpowder is a handy item that's needed to craft many volatile items and blocks: TNT, fireworks and fire charges. It's also needed to brew splash potions. If a creeper is killed by a skeleton's arrow, it will drop a random music disc to play in a jukebox.

TNT
Gunpowder is a key ingredient in everyone's favorite explosive block – the other is sand.

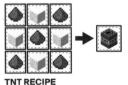

TNT RECIPE

SPAWNS
Anywhere in the Overworld on blocks of under light level 8 and in witch huts.

DROPS WHEN DEFEATED

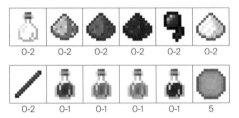

| 0-2 | 0-2 | 0-2 | 0-2 | 0-2 | 0-2 |

| 0-2 | 0-1 | 0-1 | 0-1 | 0-1 | 5 |

Witches will drop a maximum of 6 items when defeated, and if they're killed while using a potion, they'll drop that, too. Their drops are useful, but the most useful is glowstone dust, which is only naturally found in the Nether. It brews potions and crafts glowstone, fireworks and the spectral arrow, which reveals its targets from behind walls.

DID YOU KNOW?
Minecraft's music, which you can play from disks that creepers drop, is by the artist C418.

WITCH FARM

This farm uses a special property of witch huts: only witches will spawn inside their 7 × 9 × 5-block area. They can take some searching, but they can produce large numbers of useful items.

Witch huts are found in swamps. Dispatch the resident witch and build a box that encloses the whole hut.

 Light as much of the surrounding area, above- and belowground, as you possibly can, or flood it to prevent other hostile mobs from being able to spawn in the area.

 Destroy the hut from within and put 2 floors with at least 2 blocks above them inside your new box. Witches will spawn on these 2 floors.

Dig a 32-block drop next to the open end of the water trench so witches are washed along it and down the hole, where they will die at the bottom. Place hoppers connected to a chest at the bottom to collect the items.

 Place a 2-block-wide line of open trapdoors along the same position on both floors so witches will fall from upper levels.

Dig a 3-block-high trench under the lower spawning floor, ensure it is 8 blocks long, and set up flowing water from one end.

YOU WILL NEED:

ENDERMAN

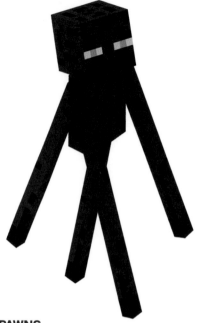

THE BOAT TECHNIQUE

Enderman farming in the Overworld is not easy. Their ability to teleport and their hatred of water means many mob farming techniques won't work. But this hunting method is somewhat safe.

1 Pick an area of open ground where you can see a long way. Arrange about 15 boats in a circle around you.

2 Light a radius of about 20 blocks around the boats to help avoid attracting the attention of other hostile mobs.

SPAWNS

In the Overworld, Nether and End, on blocks with a light level of under 8. In the Overworld they are rare, appearing in groups of between 1 and 4, and in the Nether they're very rare.

DROPS WHEN DEFEATED

0-1   5

When thrown, ender pearls will teleport players, and are also used to craft the eye of ender, an item that helps locate End portals in strongholds. Eyes of ender sometimes break when used. You'll need up to 12 to insert into the End portal in order to activate it.

3 Wait for nightfall and look for endermen. Note that they will not spawn in rain. Look directly at their eyes to anger them. When they come toward you to attack they will get caught in the boat, making it easier to hit them.

4 Endermen will teleport from the boat when you attack them, and they can attack you while they sit, so take care – a good suit of armor is advised.

BOAT

Boats are cheap and easy to make, requiring just wood planks and a wooden shovel.

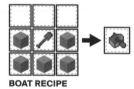

BOAT RECIPE

YOU WILL NEED:

ENDERMITE TRAP

Another technique uses the fact endermen hate endermites, but a warning: setting it up consumes the very ender pearls you're collecting.

1 Prepare a name tag for the endermite with an anvil. The name tag will prevent it from despawning.

2 At ground level, build a 3-block-high tower, place a rail on top, and place a minecart on it. The endermite is going to sit in this minecart.

3 Place a ring of trapdoors around the base of the tower and dig a 43-block-deep trench down from them. The drop will kill the endermen.

4 Place a block above the minecart and build a 2-block-deep 1 x 1 bowl above it. Stand on the edge and throw ender pearls toward the opposite edge. You'll teleport to the other side, losing a little health. Repeat, healing as necessary. It will take an average of 20 throws until the endermite appears in the bowl.

5 Quickly name tag the endermite and then destroy the block below so it falls into the minecart, and destroy all the other blocks you placed around your tower so it's all tidy.

6 Wait in a safe place nearby for endermen to spawn, attempt to attack the endermite, and fall to their deaths.

YOU WILL NEED:

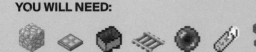

NETHER MOBS

Every mob you'll meet in the Nether is highly dangerous, but they drop rare and valuable items, many of which are essential for brewing potions. Let's take a look at each mob and how it can be farmed so you can collect drops.

MAGMA CUBE

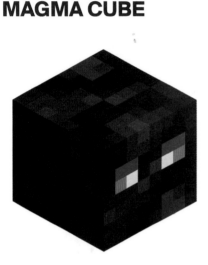

SPAWNS

In one of three different sizes, at any light level, anywhere in the Nether. They're more commonly found around Nether fortresses.

DROPS WHEN DEFEATED

0-1	1-4

Magma cream is needed to brew potions of fire resistance, which make the Nether a lot easier to explore.

ZOMBIE PIGMAN

SPAWNS

Common in the Nether, zombie pigmen spawn in groups of 4, on any solid blocks, at any light level. They can also rarely spawn on Nether portals in the Overworld.

DROPS WHEN DEFEATED

0-1	0-1	0-1	1	5-12

Zombie pigmen are a good source of gold; 9 nuggets craft into a gold ingot, or craft golden carrots, which tame horses and brew into potions of night vision, and glistering melons, which brew potions of healing. They also have a chance of dropping their gold swords, which can be smelted into a gold nugget.

ZOMBIE PIGMAN GOLD RUNS

This technique requires a little effort, but it's reliable and very easy to set up, and you can therefore start using it as soon as you arrive in the Nether. For a more advanced farm, see pages 66-67.

For a more advanced farm, see pages 66-67.

1 Find an area of Nether that has a good deal of flat space and easily connects to one or more nearby areas.

2 In each area build a 3 x 3 cobblestone shelter on open ground that leaves a 2-block-high space inside for you stand in, with wooden gates in each of the faces so you can get in and out.

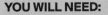

3 Once zombie pigmen have spawned into an area, carefully attack one of them and run back to your shelter. It will call out, causing all nearby pigmen to attack you.

5 Once all pigmen are killed, collect their items and move on to your next shelter to repeat the process. Be sure none are hiding behind the pillars of your shelter!

4 Ensure the gate is closed behind you and stand in the precise middle so the pigmen can't reach you, and attack them with your sword.

YOU WILL NEED:

WITHER SKELETON

SPAWNS

In groups of up to 5 in Nether fortresses at a light level of under 8.

DROPS WHEN DEFEATED

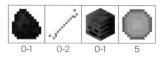

0-1	0-2	0-1	5

Wither skeletons' real value is their skull. It only has a 2.5% chance of dropping, but it helps summon the fearsome wither. From the wither you get Nether stars, which are necessary to create beacons.

Wither skeletons spawn in specific locations in and around Nether fortresses. A good place for a farm is on an open intersection, because it grants a large, flat area. The very best locations are in fortresses standing over lava, because lava prevents mobs spawning nearby.

SIMPLE WITHER SKELETON FARM

Building in the Nether is dangerous and difficult, but this simple farm helps to make collecting wither skeleton skulls safer.

1 Wither skeletons will spawn 9 blocks from the middle of the intersection, including into its corners, so build a square 20-block-wide platform centered on the intersection.

2 Destroy nearby areas of fortress and cover as much exposed ground around it as you can with slabs or glass to prevent mobs spawning elsewhere.

YOU WILL NEED:

Wither skeletons also spawn below the top of the platform. To maximize your farm's output, build a second floor underneath with a 3-block-high gap. Wither skeletons only spawn in the dark, so do not light the area with torches.

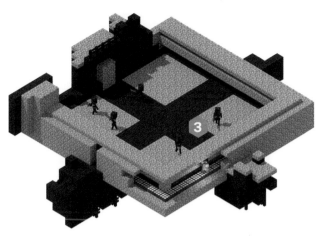

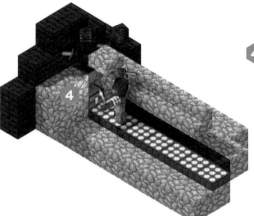

4 Build a corridor around the edge of the spawning space, using daylight sensors for the floor and stairs to make the wall looking into the space. The daylight sensors allow you to stand at a height at which only tall wither skeletons can see you, but they can't hit you.

5 Now lure wither skeletons to the end of the corridor, where they will climb the steps so you can kill them. Their items are automatically collected by the hoppers. If too many other types of mobs spawn, move away for a while and wait for them to despawn before returning.

DAYLIGHT SENSOR
Since you're in the Nether, it's easy to find Nether quartz, which you'll need to craft a daylight sensor.

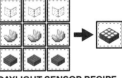

DAYLIGHT SENSOR RECIPE

TIP >

A good block to use in Nether constructions is cobblestone, because it withstands ghast fireballs. See page 72 for more info.

BLAZE

BLAZE SPAWNER FARM

This farm is built around a blaze spawner you can find in Nether fortresses. It takes a lot of dangerous building, but it generates blaze rods at a fantastic rate. It also generates a great deal of experience points very quickly.

1 Find a blaze spawner in a Nether fortress. They're often on the open top of towers. The best locations are enclosed so ghasts can't attack while you're hard at work.

SPAWNS

From spawners in Nether fortresses at a light level of under 12.

DROPS WHEN DEFEATED

| 0-1 | 10 |

Blaze rods craft brewing stands, opening up a world of potions to you. They're also crucial for making blaze powder, which is needed to craft eyes of ender. It also crafts fire charges and magma cream, which drops directly from magma cubes.

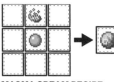

MAGMA CREAM
Brew magma cream with awkward potions to make potions of fire resistance.

MAGMA CREAM RECIPE

MOJANG STUFF

The blaze went through a few iterations before we settled on the design. Our early attempts lacked a sense of personality - then we added eyes and it suddenly felt a lot more alive. From then on, it was decided that all mobs need eyes!

YOU WILL NEED:

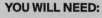

Your first task is to stop the spawner from spawning blazes so you can work. Quickly cover the platform with torches to slow their spawning down, then build out a 9 x 9 x 2 area around and on top of the spawner to disable it.

Be very careful at this stage - there's lava below you and you don't want to fall in. Try building a staircase down the side as you go.

You'll need to destroy the rest of the Nether brick underneath the spawner to create space below the spawner.

63

4 Build around the spawner to create a room with an internal space of 9 x 9 x 12 blocks. There should be 2 blocks between the spawner and the center of the ceiling.

5 Cut a 3-block channel along the center of the floor and create the corridors below that the blazes will sink down into, and from which you'll kill them.

HOW DOES IT WORK?

The height of the room allows you to be within range of the spawner while maximizing the space in which blazes can spawn. Mobs can't see through iron bars so the blazes won't be able to see you, and the cobwebs stop them from drifting out.

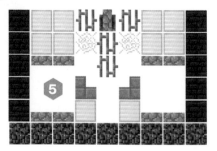

Destroy the blocks that are disabling the spawner and quickly go into the two side walkways below, because blazes will immediately spawn. As they float down, kill them with your sword. Watch for rods that sometimes fall into the central walkway.

GHAST

SPAWNS

In the Nether on solid blocks at any light level, but they are rare, spawning 20 times less frequently than other mobs.

DROPS WHEN DEFEATED

| 0-2 | 0-1 | 5 |

Ghast tears can be brewed with an awkward potion to create potions of regeneration. When crafted with glass and an eye of ender, they also craft the End crystal, which, when placed on the top of the pillars in the End, will respawn the ender dragon.

GHAST FARM

Ghasts are hard to farm effectively because they are so rare and float in the air. This farm ensures they spawn safely inside and nowhere else. It's a lot of work to build, but will also gain you gold and XP from zombie pigmen.

1 The biggest challenge is finding a good site. The ghast's rarity means it's vital that they spawn in your farm and not outside it. Find a large lava lake and cover all other ground up to a distance of around 100 blocks around the farm with slabs.

2 Build a large 4-block-high cage with open windows high above the lava. You can make multiple floors. At ceiling level place slabs every 5 blocks to prevent ghasts from escaping.

3 Place iron bars across the windows to prevent ghasts from escaping and also from seeing you. Place slabs along the bottom to prevent ghasts from pushing pigmen to the edge.

4 On upper floors, create steps so pigmen from upper floors can jump down 3 blocks to the lower one.

5 Place trapdoors in front of the middle window and create a 24-block drop trap for zombie pigmen below, with hoppers to collect their gold.

6 Build a cobblestone bridge that leads to the trapdoors and a shelter at the end, around 25 blocks away from the farm, where you can wait for ghasts to spawn.

YOU WILL NEED:

7 Many zombie pigmen will spawn on both floors. To clear them, shoot one with a bow from the safety of your bridge. All nearby pigmen will swarm toward you, falling down the hole.

8 Get a bow and a stock of arrows and, from your shelter, shoot them at ghasts as they spawn. It should take 2 shots to kill them. Run into the farm to collect their tears; since zombie pigmen are neutral they won't attack, but watch out for magma cubes occasionally spawning.

BLOCK FARMING

Some Minecraft constructions require thousands of blocks. Here we'll learn how to create large quantities fast so you don't have to hunt them down in your world. Whether you need cobblestone or cactus, wood or Nether wart, these farms will allow you to build big projects more quickly.

PRINCIPLES OF BLOCK FARMING

We can use the way in which some blocks reproduce to make big stocks of useful items. Some grow very similarly to the crops we explored earlier (see pages 12-13), though their produce isn't edible.

LOCATION

Blocks like ice and snow only form in specific biomes, so you may need to set out on expeditions to find them. Consider using Nether portals to make traveling between your main base and your special farms easier.

ENCHANTMENT

Many block farms are limited by how fast you can mine. Gold pickaxes are the fastest, but they wear out very quickly. Consider investing in enchantments like efficiency, fortune and unbreaking.

TOOLS

Some blocks only drop their item when destroyed with a specific tool. Obsidian needs a diamond pickaxe, vines can only be collected with shears, and ice requires a tool enchanted with silk touch.

SITE

If you're building a big project, it might be a good idea to position a farm making the items you're using to build, like cobblestone, nearby. Or, if it's in the Nether, close to a portal so you can bring resources in quickly.

BLOCKS

From wood to obsidian, these blocks are frequently used in building and are easy to farm if you know how. Let's take a look at what they can be used for and how to farm them efficiently.

COBBLESTONE

Cobblestone is the commonest building material, due to its strength and how easy it is to find. It's particularly effective in the Nether, because it can withstand ghast and blaze fireballs. But mining it from the ground is time-consuming and sometimes dangerous.

COBBLESTONE GENERATOR

You can mine cobblestone at speed, without even moving, using lava's ability to create cobblestone when it flows into water.

 The generator creates a 5-block line of cobblestone, which is the same length reach you have with your pickaxe.

 Hoppers collect the cobblestone as you mine it and feed it to a chest.

 An observer block detects when you mine the farthest cobblestone block, triggering a line of pistons at the top to push the top layer of generated cobblestone down. This creates a space for water and lava from the two reservoirs to flow into each other, making a new layer of cobblestone in its place.

YOU WILL NEED:

OBSIDIAN

One of the strongest blocks, obsidian can't be destroyed by creepers or TNT blasts, so it can protect important constructions. It also builds the Nether portal. But it's relatively rare and can only be mined with a diamond pickaxe.

SIMPLE OBSIDIAN GENERATOR

Obsidian is produced when flowing water moves into a lava source block, replacing that lava source block. Making it means collecting lava into lots of buckets. But this simple machine makes the final steps easier.

1 Craft buckets and gather lava into them. You'll get 1 obsidian block for each bucket of lava. Place the lava buckets into the dispenser, which carries a maximum of 9.

2 Press the button and obsidian will appear next to the dispenser. Mine it and press the button for a new obsidian block. Sometimes an empty bucket will be dispensed; just collect it and press the button again until lava is dispensed.

TIP

The Nether is a good source of lava, so if you need lots of obsidian, consider building a Nether portal next to your generator to give you an easy source of lava.

YOU WILL NEED:

SNOW

Snow falls in cold biomes, settling on the tops of blocks. When destroyed with a shovel, it drops snowballs. Snowballs can be thrown, causing no more than knockback on most mobs, but do 1.5 hearts of damage to blazes. They can also be crafted into a block of snow.

SNOWBALL FARM

Snow golems instantly generate snow on the ground they're touching, as long as they're in a cold biome. This snow can then be used to make snowballs.

 The hoppers are connected to each other. Drop an item into one of them and they will put out a pulsing signal.

 Make your snow golem here by placing 2 blocks of snow on top of each other, and a pumpkin on top.

3 Stand on the pressure plate to activate the piston.

4 This piston pushes the snow off the golem's base into snowballs. Don't worry, it doesn't harm the golem.

MOJANG STUFF

Ice is super useful for building high-speed transport systems thanks to a bug - sorry, *feature* - in the calculation of ground friction. Enclose an icy runway in a 2-block-high tunnel, and you can sprint-jump along it at a searing 16 blocks a second!

YOU WILL NEED:

  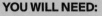

ICE

Ice forms on water directly under the sky in biomes where snow settles. When laid as a long track it can make water, mobs and players move faster, and if under soul sand, it will enhance its slowing effect. Pickaxes break ice the fastest, but ice only drops when the tool is enchanted with silk touch (see page 49).

ICE FARM

After harvesting the ice, the water flows back into the pool so it freezes again. The pool can be as big as you like.

 Freezing transforms water blocks into ice.

2 The water source blocks are directly under cover, which prevents ice forming on them, so they automatically refill the pool after harvest.

NETHER WART

Naturally found in Nether fortresses, Nether wart grows anywhere at any light level on soul sand. It's needed to brew awkward potion, which is the base for many key potions, including fire resistance, healing, night vision, strength and many more.

NETHER WART FARM

You have to replant Nether wart manually after harvesting, so this farm just harvests it automatically for you. You can extend by adding lower tiers.

 Plant from the central pathway. You should be able to reach the far blocks without having to walk on the soul sand.

 Pull the lever to release water that breaks the Nether wart when mature.

 The water flows to the hoppers very slowly because it's over soul sand!

WOOD

Wood is an excellent building material and fuel, and also crafts many vital items, so a stock of trees is essential if no forest is nearby. Planted in dirt or podzol with a light level of 8 or more, saplings will grow into trees in around 1 Minecraft day, depending on the species. They grow anywhere, including caves, the Nether and the End, provided they have at least 4 blocks clear above them.

ACACIA

Acacia is only found in savannas. It has a good yield, but it's a tricky shape for harvesting.

BIRCH

Birch grows quickly and leaves grow higher for easy harvesting, but wood yield is low.

DARK OAK

Dark oak is the fastest-growing wood, drops apples, and a thick trunk means lots of wood, but it requires 4 saplings to plant.

JUNGLE

Jungle trees are huge, which means lots of wood, but they also need plenty of space to grow.

OAK

Oak is common and drops apples and lots of saplings, but its many leaves can slow harvesting.

SPRUCE

Spruce are common but tall, making reaching their tops difficult. Saplings must be placed 2 blocks apart.

EFFICIENT LAYOUT

This layout uses 61 saplings of any type except spruce, 23 torches and 117 blocks. If lit well, as shown here, saplings will grow right next to one another. The yield isn't as high as trees growing far apart, but they're easy to harvest.

YOU WILL NEED:

VINES

Found in jungles and swamps, vines can only be gathered with shears. They craft moss stone and mossy stone bricks, and when placed against solid blocks they can be climbed. They will also break falls.

SIMPLE VINE FARM

Build this design as long as you like to maximize its output.

1 The vines grow down from the top of the structure.

2 Shear the vines as they grow downward from the marked position, from where you won't accidentally destroy the seeding vines at the top of each row.

CACTUS

This prickly block grows in sand in deserts and mesas in a similar fashion to sugar canes, except it doesn't require water. It damages any mob or player that touches it, so it can be a useful form of defense.

CACTUS FARM

This farm can be enlarged as much as you like, upward or across. It uses the fact that when a cactus grows into a space next to another block the new cactus block instantly breaks.

1 This farm uses fence posts, which also help prevent the broken cactus items from falling on to live ones and being destroyed.

2 The water below then washes them into hoppers connected to a chest.

YOU WILL NEED:

FINAL WORDS

Well done! You're now a master farmer. You can sit back and enjoy the fruits of your labor, with almost everything you could ever need at your fingertips. With all those riches, you can go out into the world, exploring even farther and building ever bigger. Your only limit is your imagination. Thanks for playing!

OWEN JONES
THE MOJANG TEAM

STAY IN THE KNOW!